IMAGES
of America

BOISE

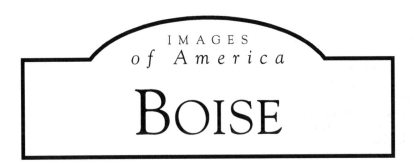

IMAGES
of America

BOISE

Frank Thomason

ARCADIA
PUBLISHING

Published by Arcadia Publishing
Charleston, South Carolina

Library of Congress Catalog Card Number: 2008933026

For all general information contact Arcadia Publishing at:
Telephone 843-853-2070
Fax 843-853-0044
E-mail sales@arcadiapublishing.com
For customer service and orders:
Toll-Free 1-888-313-2665

Visit us on the Internet at www.arcadiapublishing.com

CONTENTS

Acknowledgments   6

Introduction   7

1.   An Oasis in the Desert   9

2.   Business and Public Buildings of Old Boise   29

3.   Historic Homes   45

4.   Out and About: Living and Working in Old Boise   61

5.   Trial and Punishment   83

6.   Education and Medicine   95

7.   Chinese and Other Minorities   109

Bibliography   127

ACKNOWLEDGMENTS

Much credit for the research, photographs, and organization of this project goes to Polly Ambrose Peterson, Ph.D. Her direct and continuous involvement and passion contributed greatly to the quality and layers of depth in the format. Acknowledgment is also extended to the following employees of the Public Archives and Research Library of the Idaho State Historical Society (ISHS): archivist Carolyn Bowler and librarians Amy Vecchione and David Matte. They provided professional assistance with a positive attitude through all phases of photograph selection and analysis.

Anyone who studies Boise history soon encounters the histories by ISHS director emeritus Arthur Hart, author of three dozen works on area and state history. Thanks to historians Hugh Hartman, Carol Lynn MacGregor, Todd Shallat, and the late Merle Wells. Thanks also to Carolyn and James Thomason, Emily Peeso, Allyn and Philip Krueger, Arthur and Esther Oppenheimer, the Warm Springs Historic District, and Boise city historian Tully Gerlach. Unless otherwise noted, all images appear courtesy of the Idaho State Historical Society. The key to the identification of other sources is: Hummel Architects (HA), Hugh Hartman (HH), Idaho Black History Museum (IBHM), Jack McGee, Idaho Power (J. McGee/IP), John May/Owyhee Plaza (J. May/OP), Library of Congress (LC), Old Boise Historic District (OBHD), Public Library System in Boise (PLS), Polly A. Peterson (PAP), Carolyn Thomason (CT), Frank Thomason (FT), Priscilla Wegers (PW), and the University of Idaho (UI).

INTRODUCTION

In June 2008, a Brookings Institution report ranked the Boise metropolitan area in the top third in the nation for productivity, social inclusiveness, and environmental sustainability. Despite its humble origins, Boise became a place to fall in love with, a veritable oasis in the desert offering unparalleled outdoor opportunities for backpackers, boaters, campers, fishermen, hikers, hunters, kayakers, skiers, and many others. Chapter 1 chronicles the origins of Boise. How the earliest settlers treated the original natives was completely in alignment with federal policies of displacement and relocation of entire tribes onto reservation lands. In 1869, army detachments accompanied large groups of Shoshone and Bannock Indians from the Boise area to the Fort Hall Reservation in southeastern Idaho. But this moral stain on our national soul that generates ambivalence has never been seriously examined. For example, Gov. Caleb Lyon, who spearheaded the signing of the Treaty of Fort Boise in late 1864, at times defended local Shoshone groups and opposed their eradication during the Snake War of 1866–1868 and at other times struck a strident, popular anti-Indian tone. Similarly, Boiseans 150 years later can acknowledge the legal and moral claims by natives to the very land they work, play, and live upon, while giving little if any thought to readdressing this historic grievance.

Idaho was fashioned by political processes and decisions that defied geography and topography. As a territory and state, Idaho is the forced marriage of three very different geographical areas, a condition that continues to plague the state's political process. The first territorial governor, William H. Wallace, organized the capital in Lewiston on July 10, 1863, while Boise was being organized. By April 14, 1864, coincidentally one year to the day prior to the assignation of President Lincoln, who had appointed Wallace as governor, 1,658 Boiseans had snatched territorial capital status from 359 Lewistonians. The latter never forgave what they later came to call "The Great State of Ada" for this action, and Lewiston has attempted to secede from Idaho many times since this action. Boise was fortunate that Lewiston rather than Idaho City, originally called West Bannock, was not the original capital, since Idaho City in the mid-1860s had a population of 5,000, surpassing even Portland, Oregon, in size, and eventually reached 7,000 before the Placer mining claims began to play out.

An estimated 54,000 emigrants passed by Boise along the Oregon Trail before the 1862 gold rush into the Boise Basin that spawned the settlement. Early Boiseans experienced isolation from other population centers and an absence of the mineral resources that inspired alternative economic activities of a mercantile class as well as development of farmlands by transforming the desert to the south and west by way of irrigation. In the 1860s, inclement weather and spring flooding helped usher in a sharp recession affecting row crop and animal farming as well as mining, and it was several years before Boise acquired and developed enough housing stock and other resources to compare favorably to older cities such as Portland.

Boise in its formative decades exhibited enough chaos and lawlessness to earn it the description of a Wild West area, and many elected officials led the charge in unscrupulousness and malfeasance. In early 1866, territorial secretary Horace C. Gilson made off with the entire territorial treasury of

$41,062 and fled to Hong Kong. That spring, territorial governor Caleb Lyon absconded with all of Idaho's Indian funds in the amount of $46,418.40. On the local level, there was near-anarchy and great resistance to the formation of a city government. For example, Boise's mayor in 1867 was still respecting a campaign pledge never to be sworn into office, as did one of four council members. A nation, territory, or community born in such confusion and criminality cannot help but exhibit their effects through the years.

Chapters 2 and 3 are collections of photographs and captions representative of the design and construction of commercial and public buildings as well as older residences and their histories. Boise's builders, including the successful and fabled firms of Tourtellotte and Hummel, Wayland and Fennell, and others, applied traditional rather than innovative forms of architecture and culture that are arguably unsuited for a desert climate such as Boise's. East Coast and Midwestern approaches, with their focus on mansions and manicured landscaping, dominated the Boise architectural scene, while other styles, including Southwestern, that might have led to adoption of hydroponic and xeriscape planning never took hold. As water becomes scarcer, Boise's future landscaping may feature a radically different approach.

Chapter 4 presents visual and textual information about the social interactions of Boiseans before and after 1900. The charm of turn-of-the-century Boise lasted for two decades as people lived, worked, and played, their lives enhanced by the electric railway trolley system that connected Boise on the extreme east end of the valley with communities to the west and north and south of the Boise River in a literal loop with Caldwell on the extreme western end. The Interurban appears as a striking feature from a Camelot we have lost. Boise mayor Dave Bieter is attempting to resurrect a trolley line in Boise's downtown core.

Chapter 5 deals with Idaho's "trial of the 20th century," the prosecution of mine union leaders for the 1905 murder of former governor Frank Steunenberg. Famed attorney Clarence Darrow won acquittals, but the trial put Boise on the map and made the reputations of prosecutors William Borah and James Hawley.

Chapter 6 concerns the impressive history of education and medicine in Boise. Organizing a public school system and modern medical facilities was slow and difficult, but today Boise can boast of an excellent educational and medical resource base, and Idahoans and others take great pride not only in St. Luke's and St. Alphonsus regional medical centers but also in the academic as well as athletic achievements of Boise State University as an institution of higher learning.

Chapter 7 describes the Chinese and other minorities in Idaho's capital city but does not tell the entire story. For example, space precluded treatment of all minorities, such as Eastern Europeans, as well as Japanese immigrants, who outnumbered the Chinese by 1910. The former were generally part of the migration waves from Europe into American and westward to Idaho in the late 19th century, while the latter are better considered in a history of Boise in the last half of the 20th century, after World War II.

One

AN OASIS IN THE DESERT

Boise is a mosaic of the traditional and the avant-garde, a blend of the razed, the restored, and the revolutionary. From its humble origins along the Oregon Trail, which ran through Main Street, to the growth spurts starting with the gold rush to the Boise Basin that brought the U.S. Army to Fort Boise, the "City of Trees" was built on a high desert plateau tumbling from the foothills of the Rocky Mountains to the north and east and featuring buildings, activities, and a population that are still expanding rapidly to points west. Early settlers after 1863 soon dislodged Shoshone and Bannock Indians from both sides of the Boise River and set about cobbling together a city and the capitol of a territory signed into existence by Pres. Abraham Lincoln.

The U.S. Army sent a detachment under Bvt. Maj./Capt. Pinckney (also spelled Pinkney) Lugenbeel from Washington Territory to establish a military presence, ostensibly to protect settlers and miners in the Boise Basin. Banking and mercantile interests clung to traditions brought from elsewhere into southwestern Idaho on their path of economic and social development. Boiseans wrested the territorial capital away from Lewiston up north and finally crafted a functioning municipal government. They also dug canals and extended the arable region to accommodate farmers to the west decades before large dams and government canal projects completed the process of reclaiming large portions of the high desert plateau that stretches to the west and south of the Rocky Mountain foothills that form Boise's northern and eastern boundaries.

Cultural amenities and progress were not easily had on the front lines of this hard-scrabble frontier. The telegraph arrived in 1874 and the telephone in 1884. The railroad finally reached Boise in 1887 via a spur line from an area 20 miles to the southwest. By the end of the 19th century, the electric railway known as the Interurban began to form a mass transit loop of service from Boise westward through several communities and back until it was forced into bankruptcy by the oil and automobile interests in 1928.

Shoshone-Bannock natives rendezvoused in warm weather along *Skam-naugh* (the Boise River) to fish, hunt, and socialize. Indian and British trappers from Fort Vancouver named the river "Boise" around 1812, long before Capt. Arthur Bonneville's party approached from the southeast in 1837, when one trapper reportedly yelled out "les Bois" as he saw the sparse stands of willows and cottonwoods along the riverbanks. Two other area streams were also given the name, but only the Boise River maintains its original French definition. Boise decades later became known as the "City of Trees" after early settlers and developers including surveyor general Lafayette Cartee and Thomas Jefferson Davis had overseen the planting of several thousand trees. The Boise River Festival began in 1991 and ended in 2003, but the river itself remains a vital conveyor of life-giving water in a high plains desert land. (PAP.)

According to Todd Shallat, original natives, who discerned the outline of a poised bird of prey among its boulders, named Castle Rock, adjacent to Table Rock, "Eagle Rock." Shoshone Indians called it *Boa-Sea*, a reference to bloating caused by white-supplied rotten apples. In 1990, a developer, Morningside Heights Partnership, submitted an application to build a 177-unit subdivision atop the ridge. Fort Hall Shoshone-Bannocks, Duck Valley Shoshone Paiutes, and the East End Neighborhood Association filed a lawsuit. A Native American leader said that excavation would "sanction the mutilation of our ancestors." The U.S. Senate never ratified the 1864 Treaty of Boise, so the natives never officially surrendered their claim to ownership. The city spent $500,000 to create a land strip buffer, East Enders chipped in $75,000, and a 1996 city council memorandum of agreement acknowledged the tribes as lawful "successors" or "descendants" of the site's original owners. (PAP.)

Displaced Shoshone and Bannock Indians and the growing number of white invaders soon came to blows. By January 1863, when a regional fort was authorized in Boise, a group of volunteers under Jefferson Standifer retaliated against local natives, wiping out one Malheur group and threatening and driving out many others. Once built, Fort Boise protected natives from hostile miners as much as it defended white settlements and roadways. In 1864, violence from mining camps in Oregon reached Idaho, and Fort Boise fulfilled its mission against the natives. Many Shoshones, shown here, went into hiding, in fear of the soldiers and white civilians with their overwhelming numbers, supplies, and arsenal. Several hundred natives were isolated northeast of the settlement, where they suffered from starvation and tuberculosis before they were herded onto wagons and in 1869 taken to Fort Hall Indian Reservation in southeastern Idaho. (PAP.)

Above, the removal of Native Americans, whose ancestors had hunted and fished along the Boise River for at least 12,000 years, guaranteed there were insufficient natives left in Boise to constitute an ethnic minority. Below, this sketch of a mural painted on a wall of the old Ada County Courthouse in Boise depicts whites about to hang a Native American. The painting dates from approximately 1940 and is a current topic of controversy among legislators utilizing the courthouse as temporary quarters during the renovation of the statehouse. The natives' treatment by white settlers is a topic that still makes many white descendants uncomfortable, a socio-psychological loose end of undetermined proportions. (Above PAP; below CT.)

Described as the "Luther Burbank" of Boise Valley by historian Hugh Hartman, Lafayette Cartee was Boise's first nurseryman and grew over 40 different types of trees from the East, Europe, and the Orient. A native of Syracuse, New York, and a former college math instructor, builder, architect, railroad superintendent and engineer, and the first surveyor general of Idaho Territory, Cartee conducted the first survey of public lands and established an initial point in the sagebrush-dotted desert 15 miles southwest of Boise where the first parallel intersected the first meridian. In Boise, he planted the first ornamental shrubs, cypress, juniper, and sycamore trees and may be described as the father of the City of Trees. He and his Pennsylvanian wife, Mary Bell, had four children; she died in 1862 at 37, and he passed away in 1891 at the age of 67.

This statue of Abraham Lincoln with the accompanying Gettysburg Address dates from 1915 and sat in front of the Idaho State Veterans Home on the grounds of old Fort Boise. Lincoln had a special relationship with Idaho, creating it as a territory and appointing its first officials. They included James H. Alvord for the office of marshal of Idaho Territory, an appointment recommended by William H. Wallace, the congressional delegate from the territory. The briefest memo Lincoln wrote on April 14, 1865, his last day on earth, was the single-word reply, "Appoint." President Lincoln himself attended the April 1863 meeting where the decision was made to name the proposed new territory "Idaho." Former lieutenant governor and attorney general David H. Leroy, chairman of the Idaho Lincoln Bicentennial Commission, has amply documented the close relationship between Lincoln and Idaho. (PAP.)

LINCOLN DAY BANQUET

FEBRUARY 13th, 1928

OWYHEE HOTEL

BOISE

On the left is a ticket to the Lincoln Day Banquet at the Owyhee Hotel in 1928. D. F. Banks presided, with College of Idaho president Dr. W. J. Boone giving the invocation. Speaker Gov. H. C. Baldridge's topic was "Our Republican Heritage." The menu included roasted Idaho turkey, Idaho potatoes, "Oh Mamma" New Jersey peas, Idaho lettuce, and asparagus tips, plus Idaho pressed-brick cream, Owyhee cake, and coffee. Below, Lincoln Bicentennial Commission chairman David Leroy (far left) watches Gov. C. L. Otter sign the proclamation in February 2008 initiating the two-year Lincoln traveling exhibit. At right are Lincoln portrayer Skip Critell and members of the Idaho Civil War Reenactors. (Above J. May/OP; below FT.)

Bvt. Maj./Capt. (later Col.) Pinckney Lugenbeel, pictured to the right, moved on to other assignments after building the fort's first structures. He and several associates were among the 20 subscribers to the new city town site, where lots were reserved. On June 1, 1863, Lugenbeel left Fort Vancouver, Washington Territory, with Companies D, G, and I of the 1st Washington Territorial Infantry. Below, on June 28, 1863, three detachments arrived at the future Camp Boise. On July 6, he selected a site for the army post at the base of the Boise foothills. He also selected wood and hay reserve sites for stock fodder and identified an area where limestone could be quarried for permanent buildings. (Above ISHS; below PAP.)

COL PINKNEY LUGENBEEL

UNITED STATES ARMY
RESERVE CENTER

Irish natives John Andrew O'Farrell, 38, and Mary Anne Chapman, 21, married in 1861 in Kentucky and migrated separately to Boise, where he drove the first corner stake of the city 40 days after arriving in 1863. In late 1864, John shot a man and was jailed in the fort's guardhouse. In 1869, he lost a claim to a section of the original town site to the city. In 1871, the family relocated to Ross Fork in Oneida County to raise stock but later returned to Boise, where O'Farrell owned farmland and promoted the original New York Canal, providing irrigation water between the Boise and Snake Rivers. The couple raised seven adopted children, including a Native American from Oregon who became a nurse, and had seven children, of whom two died as infants. One surviving daughter and her son served time for embezzling city funds.

The humble cabin above was built by Irish émigré John O'Farrell in the summer of 1863. His wife, Mary Anne, hailed two priests riding by on their way to Oregon. Fathers Theodore Mesplie and A. Z. Poulin conducted the first local religious services in the O'Farrell cabin. Father Mesplie visited Boise regularly to serve Catholics in the new town and from Fort Boise. John built the family's first residence on the corner of Fifth and Franklin Streets. In 1892, O'Farrell built the impressive two-story white brick residence below at 420 West Franklin Street, with its fence of material salvaged from the old Dewey Palace in Nampa. Its Victorian garden features a French gazebo. John was involved in a project to build a dam on the Boise River to create an irrigation canal. (Both PAP.)

The earliest known image of Boise is this oil painting from 1864 by carriage painter Arn Hincelin of downtown looking eastward to Table Rock. Most buildings of adobe and wood rather than brick were susceptible to the fires that plagued early communities. The covered wagon is symbolic of the freight lines carrying supplies from Boise to Idaho City and Placerville to support gold mining in the Boise Basin. Below, Boise's earliest map is dated 1864 and depicts business locations with a list of owners. (Above ISHS; below HH.)

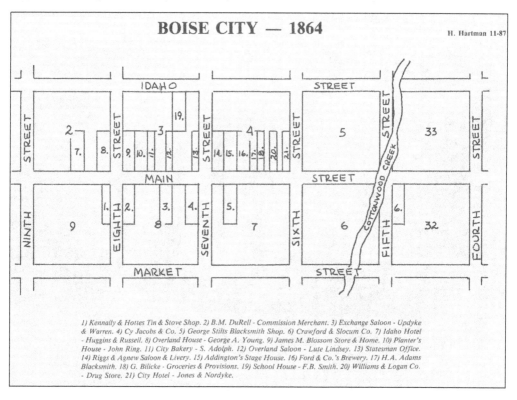

BOISE CITY — 1864

H. Hartman 11-87

1) Kennally & Hottes Tin & Stove Shop. 2) B.M. DuRell - Commission Merchant. 3) Exchange Saloon - Updyke & Warren. 4) Cy Jacobs & Co. 5) George Stilts Blacksmith Shop. 6) Crawford & Slocum Co. 7) Idaho Hotel - Huggins & Russell. 8) Overland House - George A. Young. 9) James M. Blossom Store & Home. 10) Planter's House - John Ring. 11) City Bakery - S. Adolph. 12) Overland Saloon - Lute Lindsey. 13) Statesman Office. 14) Riggs & Agnew Saloon & Livery. 15) Addington's Stage House. 16) Ford & Co.'s Brewery. 17) H.A. Adams Blacksmith. 18) G. Bilicke - Groceries & Provisions. 19) School House - F.B. Smith. 20) Williams & Logan Co. - Drug Store. 21) City Hotel - Jones & Nordyke.

The undated photograph of Boise shown above was probably taken in the early 1860s. Stagecoaches and supply wagons ferried passengers and supplies between Boise and the mining camps to the northeast. Paved streets didn't arrive in Boise until the 1890s. Many a passenger, bone-weary from a jangling overland trip from places such as Kelton, Utah, 264 miles to the southeast, viewed Boise with great delight. This 19th-century hitching post at 1308 Warm Springs Avenue is one of several such surviving items along the boulevard. The attached livery and carriage shop were removed or converted, leaving these small concrete pillars as evidence of an equestrian era when wagons and horses were tethered to the iron ring affixed to the top. (Above ISHS; below PAP.)

The earliest known photograph of Main Street was taken in 1866 from a porch looking west at Sixth and Main Streets. It depicts freight wagons, oxen and mule teams, and false fronts typically associated with Wild West architectural styles. Note the unpaved street and the caravan of covered wagons proceeding down a crowded thoroughfare. Below, local historian Hugh Hartman drew this interesting map from a survey conducted by Peter Bell in the fall of 1867. It provides an early description of land and soil, as well as cottonwood and willow trees along the south bank of the Boise River. It also shows the army wood and hay reserves that served the needs of city residents and Fort Boise to the north. (Above ISHS; below HH.)

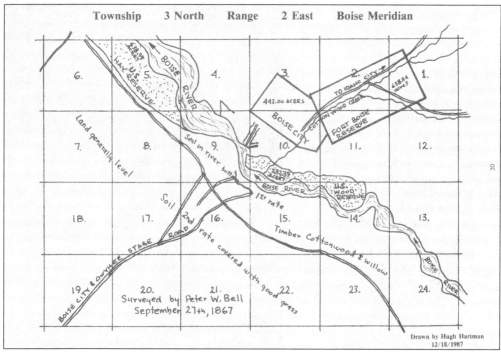

The 1895 street scene above, prior to pavement and motorized vehicles, shows many downtown businesses, including a blacksmith, hardware, second-hand store, and side-by-side a wagon shop and John Atkinson's Horse Shoeing. A. B. Mullet of the U.S. Treasury Department designed the 1872 U.S. Assay Office, below, as an Italianate cube topped with a cupola. Between 1872 and 1933, millions of dollars in gold and silver passed through the building, which became the district headquarters of the U.S. Forest Service in 1933. Now a National Landmark, in 1973 it was entrusted to the State of Idaho and its historical society. (Above ISHS; below PAP.)

Boise was platted on a high desert plateau that abuts the foothills. Large projects such as the New York Canal had to wait until government resources could be applied around 1900. In 1906, a water-users association agreed to a value to $14 per acre for previous canals and upgrades, leading to a major diversion dam, giving access to A. D. Foote's dormant New York Canal, the building of Diversion Dam in 1909, and two years later, the construction of Arrowrock storage dam. Early local canals were expanded starting in 1864, with legislative action incorporating a community ditch company on December 21. Expenses involved in enlarging the river's main channel northward eventually proved overwhelming to private resources. In 1877, William Morris extended a 7-mile canal onto bench land south of downtown. Irrigation transformed the Treasure Valley.

The railroad's arrival was delayed for 20 years by the national financial panic of 1884 and local wrangling. A new consortium of developers of a railway town site in 1886 promoted a route along Indian Creek between Caldwell and Kuna. Nampa developer James A. McGee convinced Boston railroad magnate J. F. Curtis of the viability of the former's Idaho Central rail connection business, incorporated on June 26, 1886. Curtis arranged financing of a rail-bed grade from Nampa to Boise, and Mormon contractors from Montpelier in southeastern Idaho finished the project in three months. The railroad reached Boise via an Idaho Central spur route from Indian Creek (Kuna) on September 3, 1887. A thousand people welcomed it, and struggling enterprises received a much-needed boost and increased opportunities. The activity generated helped lead to Idaho statehood three years later in 1890.

Firefighters proudly parade with horse-drawn wagons at flag-draped South and Main Streets around 1911 in *Statesman* photographer George Russell's picture. The Boise Fire Department has participated in many parades since. The first volunteer fire department was formed in 1876 and soon grew into a first-rate force of firefighters on the frontier. By the beginning of the 20th century, civic pride was evident in downtown Boise, as shown in this photograph of Mr. and Mrs. Claud Sherwood and their two children. They are being transported in a horse-drawn carriage pictured in front of the Owyhee Hotel in 1901. Note the horses' elegant tack. (Above ISHS; below OBHD.)

Mr. and Mrs. Claud Sherwood and two children in carriage on Main Street, Boise, in front of the Owyhee Hotel; 1901. ISHS 81-32.6

Thomas Jefferson Davis was born on January 2, 1838, in Cincinnati, Ohio. He and his brother, Frank, were orphaned and bound to a wealthy Monmouth farmer, and at age 23, he and Frank crossed the plains with their own mule team in a company of 75 men. In December 1862, they settled in the Boise Basin, where Tom soon netted a tidy profit for potatoes, onions, and cabbages on 360 government acres on the north side of the Boise River and from 7,000 trees costing $1.25 each. On April 26, 1871, he married a gracious Canadian émigré, Julia McCrum, the housekeeper for a Boise doctor. They had six children and built a 12-room frame residence at 415 South Seventh Street. "Quiet Tom," as he was known, was a skilled violinist who played in the Boise City band. Julia and Tom sold produce to travelers on the Oregon Trail.

Julia McCrum Davis was born on January 24, 1847, in Waterloo, Galt County, Canada West. She died on September 19, 1907, and was interred in the Pioneer Cemetery. Her husband of 36 years, Thomas Jefferson Davis, passed away on June 10, 1908, and was laid to rest alongside his cherished spouse. The Julia Davis 2002 Memorial in the southeast end of the Rose Garden in the park that bears her name was sculpted in bronze by Jerry Snodgrass and depicts her offering an apple to a pioneer girl. Husband Tom donated the former apple orchard site to the city for the park. (Above ISHS; below PAP.)

Two

BUSINESS AND PUBLIC BUILDINGS OF OLD BOISE

Boise evolved from a culture of early self-consciousness of inferiority to larger, more established cities such as Portland to the west and from a rough-and-tumble Wild West atmosphere to one of civilization and respectability. The first merchants lived and worked in buildings with walls made of wood board and batten, entryways cut from canvas and cloth, and rough-hewn timber or even dirt floors complemented outside by unpaved streets.

The archeology of Old Boise reveals individuals and groups yearning to establish "mass" or substance in their buildings, searching for permanence that was expressed in styles or statements of values imported mainly from back East and places in between. Those styles tended to include Greek and Romanesque, Gothic with touches of medieval and Renaissance, and even Mediterranean and Moorish elements before the art deco period of the 1930s and later styles. All expressed a statement of settlement and a determination to bring services into a state capital striving to succeed and impress.

When famed attorney Clarence Darrow visited Boise shortly after 1900 to defend accused assassins in the Steunenberg murder case, he was impressed enough with Boise's buildings, both businesses and residences, to refer to the evolving capital as "the Athens of the desert." He could also have described it as a hodgepodge or, in gentler terms, as a growing city characterized by an evolving architecture of eclecticism. Eventually, all surviving buildings become archeology, and the ruination and remnants retreat from a distance into a broken outline of earlier eras.

The late 20th century saw functionality and size replace earlier architectural styles and values. Boise's misnamed "downtown redevelopment" process of the 1960s and 1970s resulted in dozens of irreplaceable buildings torn down in the name of urban renewal, but fortunately enough, adjacent aged buildings survived to create the historic preservation districts or overlays of Warm Springs Avenue and the North End, among others. A building is much more than its material and design. It is an expression of life of bygone eras.

Connecticut native John Tourtellotte (left) was a self-educated architect and promoter who arrived in Idaho in 1890. German native Charles Frederick Hummel (below) was a formally trained architect who arrived in Idaho in 1895. Five years later, Tourtellotte opened his own office; in 1910, Tourtellotte and Hummel was formed. The firm developed extensive residential and commercial client lists in Idaho and neighboring states, but their strongest institutional base remained in Boise, where the firm designed over 30 buildings for the Diocese of Boise in over 40 years as well as state-funded institutions, including the University of Idaho. Their local legacy includes the Idaho State Capitol and St. John's Cathedral. (Above ISHS; below HA.)

The image above shows the Idaho Territorial Capitol between Central School and the Ada County Courthouse before 1890. Below, Tourtellotte and Company secured its reputation with the design of the Idaho State Capitol, which began in 1905, with the wings completed in 1919. John Tourtellotte described it as a "plucky little dome seen egg-smooth against the large, bare hills of the Boise Front" that comported with the national model in Washington, D.C. The exterior sandstone was quarried in the nearby foothills, with material for a granite base shipped from Vermont. The structure is undergoing extensive basement expansion to increase space for legislative offices in 2009. (Both ISHS.)

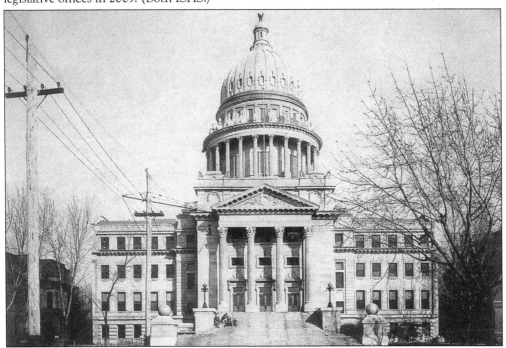

On the left, a dapper John Tourtellotte, complete with bowler hat, surveys the view from the dome of the Idaho State Capitol around 1910. A talented salesman, he compared the Idaho statehouse in local press articles with more grandiose examples of Roman architecture such as St. Peter's in Rome, St. Paul's in London, and our own U.S. Capitol in Washington, D.C. The aerial photograph below, taken after 1919, when both wings of the capitol were completed, shows what Tourtellotte described as a grand, majestic building with powerful outlines, yet possessing refinement and beauty in the details of its sculpture. (Above ISHS; below J. McGee/IP.)

The old city hall, built in 1893 on the southeast corner of Eighth and Idaho Streets, was a source of great civic pride described as a red brick and sandstone castle in the Romanesque architectural style. It boasted five stories, cost $50,000, and brought together under one roof all city offices, a four-cell city jail, and the firehouse. The new sewer system in 1894 cost almost as much as the new city building. In 1953, the irreplaceable 60-year-old structure, designed by German-trained architect John C. Paulsen, fell to the wrecking ball, and a Skaggs drugstore was built in its place. Officials built a new city hall at Capitol Boulevard and Main Street, where a former district of bawdy houses lay in ruins. *Harper's Weekly*, writes Shallat, said that Boise was possibly on its way to becoming "the first American city to have deliberately eradicated itself."

The landmark Idanha Hotel was designed by William Stewart Campbell for John and Thomas McMillan and was considered Boise's downtown showcase on the northeast corner of Tenth and Main Streets. In 1891, Peter Sonna bought the Presbyterian church on that site and then sold the land for $5,000 to the Idanha Hotel Company, which built a five-story hotel of cut stone and pressed brick with three round towers. It later added a story to become Boise's first six-story building and to inspire a succession of buildings of similar or greater height. The erection of the Idanha inspired four other buildings with a half-dozen stories in the ensuing decade. It symbolized ebullience and progressivism in a material sense that characterized the world at the end of the 19th century. Today, the Idanha has been converted to a private apartment building.

The building on the right, renamed Eastman in 1927, was formerly the Overland Building, designed by Tourtellotte and Company on the site of the 1864 Overland House. The firm fashioned a four-story palazzo in Second Renaissance Revival style with top-floor rounded windows beneath a cornice of terra-cotta and festooned with smiling lions' heads. The building fell victim to arson on the night of January 23, 1987. Below, the site was an open-air market for street vendors and is the infamous "hole" defying efforts of developers. The city has allowed a painted wooden wall as a temporary cover for the once-proud element of the city's heart. (Above ISHS; below PAP.)

Above, the six-story Owyhee Hotel was begun in 1909 and opened in 1910 on the southwest corner of Eleventh and Main Streets. It helped usher in the city's skyscraper period. Regarded as the city's finest hostelry, it boasted a roof garden with a view of the foothills to the northeast. Below, the hotel lobby featured plush, comfortable furnishings for guests and an ornate balcony and railing extending around the second floor. Romanesque columns literally and figuratively anchored this two-story interior scene. An early hotel receipt indicates a room cost $3.50 per day and a meal cost between $1 and $1.30. (Both J. May/OP.)

Above, Frank R. Coffin constructed the three-story brick Pioneer Building on the southeast corner of Eighth and Main Streets in 1894. The 1864 B. M. DuRell building made way for the more "modern" structure designed by a local architect and revised by K. K. Cutter of Spokane, Washington. Coffin had been a young employee in the firm of Twitchell and Moody, which operated a hardware and tin shop in the DuRell building. The Pioneer Building featured a prancing horse on its roof with the word "Harness" in capital letters. The early photograph below shows Pioneer Tent and Awning conducting a brisk business in canvas goods. (Both OBHD.)

The Overland Hotel, built in 1864 at Eighth and Main Streets and depicted above in 1885, operated until 1905. In 1893, horses tethered outside sent foul odors into the dining room, generating a conflict between the owners and the draymen who, similar to today's taxicabs, parked outside, awaiting new customers. The first cold water system in town was developed to serve this early hotel. R. Z. Johnson built the law office below at 112 North Sixth Street in 1885. He had been a successful attorney in Silver City in Owyhee County. The building's overall shape is Greek Revival, but the trio of cylindrical columns made of wood is actually anticlassical and reveal a predilection for cast iron that was then popular. Johnson boasted one of the finest law libraries in the Territory of Idaho. (Above ISHS; below OBHD.)

The first joint project of John Tourtellotte and Charles Hummel was the 1900–1901 downtown Union Block on Idaho Street. Characterized by a rough facade and massive arches, the two-story Richardsonian Romanesque sandstone office building below, costing $35,000, was also a dancing academy. The developers included Moses Alexander and former Boise Barracks commandant Gen. John Green. Former mayor and governor Moses Alexander erected his "big white store" at the corner of Ninth and Main Streets in 1924 after two terms as governor. The white, terra-cotta surface is weather resistant. The owner traveled east to gather input from professional architects, but Tourtellotte and Hummel's design included plush exterior fabric materials of imported buffed terra-cotta and long rows of display windows that presaged the Egyptian Theater. (Above ISHS; below LC.)

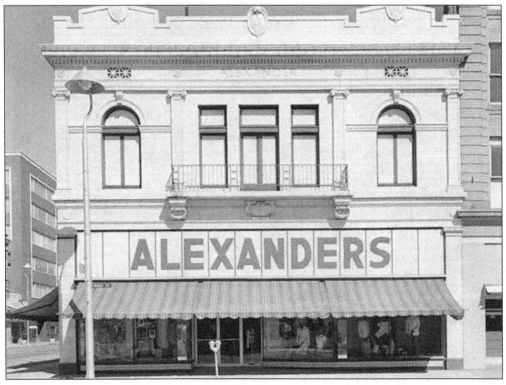

The discovery of the tomb of King Tut in 1922 generated a national craze for ancient Egypt. Above, the Egyptian Theater opened in Boise in 1927, when sound films were supplanting silent movies. The theater features a red tile roof and a smooth exterior and is the only surviving silent-era movie house in Boise with a pipe organ. Its exterior complements the Alexander Building. Architect Frederick Hummel studied at the University of Pennsylvania and visited Graumann's Egyptian Theater, for which Boise's theater was named, and the Metropolitan Museum in New York. Pictured below inside, huge circular columns and reproductions of visuals and hieroglyphics await theatergoers. (Both ISHS.)

Boise's premiere land developer, Walter E. Pierce, built Hotel Boise (right), which was completed in 1930. It sat only one block from the state capitol, and its 10 stories dwarfed all other downtown buildings. Its design was art deco, signaling a new period in area architecture. Soon thereafter, large neon signs were anchored on top of the building, but they were removed in the 1970s when a restaurant was added. The plans were drawn in Tourtellotte and Hummel's Portland office, and Frank Hummel was the designer. Below, the impressive interior consisted mainly of brass, glass, and abstract ornamentation. Its ballroom boasts fluted Ionic pilasters and friezes, all in a modern form that complements its classic origins and tastes. (Both ISHS.)

Five-time mayor James Pinney (above) ran pack trains to mines in Oregon, Colorado, and Idaho. He was also a stationer, bookseller, and theatrical producer and a postmaster in Bannock (later Idaho City) before moving in 1873 to Boise, where he opened City Book Store and built a mansion for his second wife, Mary Rogers. Pinney's Columbia Theater (below) opened in 1893 with a production of Shakespeare's *As You Like It*. Designed by John C. Paulsen, it blended features of Medieval Europe with elements of Mediterranean or even Moorish architecture. In 1908, Pinney tore it down to accommodate the larger Pinney Theater. (Both ISHS.)

The Elks Building at Ninth and Jefferson Streets is adjacent to Capitol Square, the political center of Idaho, and on the north edge of the city's Central Business District. By 1907, this area also housed the Boise Valley Railroad Company office and trolley waiting room at 810 Bannock Street. On June 14, 1907, the Fraternal Order of Elks decided to build a new hall that would favorably reflect upon their growing organization. It was long uncertain whether the building would have two or four stories, and it took six years before the cornerstone of a new temple was laid on September 29, 1913. The cornerstone was only 10 feet from the Pinney Theater, allowing a private alleyway between the structures. On May 26, 1914, several thousand Boiseans came together for opening ceremonies and a grand ball. (OBHD and J. May/OP.)

Above, Milton Hamilton is inside and Robert Reynolds is outside the first *Statesman* newspaper office at Seventh and Idaho Streets, where the first issue was published on July 26, 1864. This two-story wood-frame building replaced an earlier adobe hut with a dirt floor. The *Statesman* was the second southwestern Idaho newspaper. Below, the *Statesman* moved into the former Bilicke Building in July 1871. In autumn of 1873, the business relocated two doors east into a brick building at Sixth and Main Streets and enjoyed frontage on two streets. The current business is on the east side of Curtis Road off I-84. (Both ISHS.)

Three

HISTORIC HOMES

Commercial structures convey more than commerce in their design and construction, and historic homes likewise symbolize far more than mere dwellings and houses. The still-existing examples of the latter in Boise were mainly due to the vision and hard work of two local firms, Tourtellotte and Hummel and its chief rival, Wayland and Fennell. Harrison Boulevard developer Walter E. Pierce hired the latter to design the historic home at 1905 North Twenty-first Street, a large two-story bungalow built in 1914 and used as the gubernatorial residence after 1947.

John Everett Tourtellotte was born in East Thompson, Connecticut, in 1869, and came by way of Colorado to Boise in 1890 at the age of 21. He reportedly pioneered the use of brick veneer in local construction. In 1900, he formed his own company, and 10 years later, he entered a partnership with Charles Frederick Hummel. The latter was born in Baden, Germany, in 1857, immigrated to the United States in 1885, and came to Boise in 1895. Unlike his partner, Hummel had been a formally trained architect in Europe and was most likely the major designer of most surviving "Italianesque eclectic" buildings the firm built in Boise between 1900 and 1920. In 1906 and 1916 respectively, his sons, Frederick and Frank, joined the company.

Residential architecture conveys a sense of majesty and importance, of style and personal taste. Boise's styles were mainly imported from back east and the Midwest, and the landscaping included manicured lawns ill suited to the southwestern Idaho desert. A building, whether commercial or residential, also makes a bold statement about its owners as filtered through its designers. Despite myths about Old West and northwestern equality, Boise like most places was very early imbued with class distinctions. Those who could afford imposing structures in which to work and live formed an oligarchy, a merchant class that soon distinguished itself from the ranks of commoners and workers whose homes either disappeared or fell into obscurity.

James H. Brady was born on June 12, 1862, in Indiana County, Pennsylvania, to John and Cathrine Lee Brady, who were of Scotch-Irish descent. His family moved to Johnson County, Kansas, where James attended district public schools and Leavenworth Normal College. He was a schoolteacher, semi-weekly newspaper editor, and realtor before moving to Pocatello in 1895. Brady promoted irrigation and helped build several canals, including one on the Fort Hall Indian Reservation. He also organized the Idaho Consolidated Power Company, a hydroelectric system in southern Idaho. In 1908, Brady was elected the eighth governor but lost his reelection bid in 1910 to Democrat James Hawley. In 1913, he was elected U.S. senator to complete the term of Weldon Heyburn, who died in 1912, and, in November 1914, to a full six-year term but died in office on January 13, 1918, in Washington, D.C.

Tourtellotte and Hummel designed this impressive three-story Queen Anne brick, stone, and shingle structure in 1897 for Alfred and Victoria Eoff. Governor Brady bought the home in December 1908 and engaged architects Wayland and Fennel to superintend its rearranging, including converting the basement into a den. Brady, a lifelong bachelor, needed a Boise residence suitable for entertainment. His sister served as housekeeper. In the fall of 1909, Brady replaced porch screens with panes of plate glass and installed natural hot-water coils. He also had coils installed on the porch for the natural hot water with which the house was heated. The space became a sun parlor by day and an enchanting moon room by night. Credit for the remodeling goes to interior decorator Marie I. D. Irvin. On sunny mornings, the governor and his niece viewed the Owyhees during breakfast. (LC.)

Tourtellotte and Hummel designed the designed the Children's Home made of sandstone in a Western Colonial Revival modified mission Roman Classical–style at 740 Warm Springs Avenue in 1910 with a low-profiled hip roof featuring exposed rafters and overhanging eaves, a raised first floor, and stone column-supported porch entry. The largest building on Warm Springs Avenue, it became a center for orphaned, homeless, neglected, and abused children after Rev. O. P. Christian in 1907 requested support for a children's home society in Idaho. Schoolteacher Cynthia Mann donated the land, and the State Legislature appropriated a building fund of $20,000, which was doubled through thousands of donations. The building still serves children as an outpatient counseling and assessment office and houses the Warm Springs Counseling Center. The mission of the Children's Home continues after a century, and the foster care system touches the lives of thousands. (PAP.)

Dr. Franz Brandt built the Prairie-style home above featuring overhanging eaves and second-story corner windows popularized by Frank Lloyd Wright at 815 Warm Springs Avenue in 1917. The overall form, low-pitched roof, and elliptical transom window suggest Federal-style influences. The three-story, 20-room home hosted musicals and receptions, and President Hoover breakfasted there. Craig Coffin, son of Boise City National Bank Pres. Frank Coffin, lived in the 1919 Colonial-style home pictured below at 829 Warm Springs Avenue until his death in 1939. New owners glassed in the porch, updated the kitchen, and added second-story chauffeur's quarters to the garage. Current owners William and Flora Skillern bought it in 1971. (Both PAP.)

Architects Wayland and Fennell designed the Georgian home above at 945 Warm Springs Avenue with elegant proportions for Charles and Margaret Davidson of the Davidson Grocery Company in 1916. They later sold it to Steen Fletcher of the Fletcher Oil Company. The house's seven owners remodeled, repainted original woodwork, and removed a large stained-glass window on the landing. It also boasts a swimming pool surrounded by formal gardens. Tourtellotte and Hummel built the 4,300-square-foot Mission-style residence below with touches of Spanish California at 1009 Warm Springs Avenue in 1911 for William Regan, whose father owned the local water company. Plain square columns replaced the original Doric ones at its entryway. Current owners Arthur and Esther Oppenheimer remodeled the kitchen and added a pergola with a fireplace. (Both PAP.)

Laura Cunningham and her husband, J. W., moved into the mansion at 1109 Warm Springs in 1916 following the death of her father, C. W. Moore, president of the hot water company, who installed geothermal heating in his own residence to demonstrate its practicality. In 1867, he was a founder of Idaho First National Bank, the second national bank west of the Mississippi River. Moore foresaw the need for standardizing currency to replace gold dust bartering, with its vulnerability to adulteration. James King designed the three-story mansion in the French chateau–style with 14 rooms featuring decorative woodwork of cherry, oak, and redwood. The Moore mansion was the first home in the United States to use geothermal water as a heat source. The sisters were neighbors who enjoyed the geothermal water that ran through the radiators and pipes of their homes. (PAP.)

John Tourtellotte designed this exquisite Queen Anne–style "Painted Lady" at 1504 Warm Springs Avenue in 1880. It was built at a cost of $2,600 for Edward Payne, Esq. Its original size was 2,200 square feet. From 1937 to 1954, the Murray Burns family remodeled and enlarged the home to 4,800 square feet, removed the front of the porch, dug a full basement, reconfigured the kitchen, added a bathroom, installed a living room fireplace, and covered the exterior with steel siding and white paint. Between 1954 and 1982, the Curtis Jones family built a 1,000-square-foot spa off the kitchen. Steve and Connie Francis removed the steel siding and restored the exterior in the early 1980s, enlarged the master bedroom, and added a master bath and a deck to the spa room. Current owners Tom and Mary Glynn Wilford are continuing the traditions of restoration. (PAP.)

Architects Wayland and Fennell designed this English Tudor home above at 1127 Warm Springs Avenue with a pitched roof, arched doorways, and leaded-glass windows. Construction was begun in 1925 by Frank Parsons and his wife, Anna Moore, sister of Laura Moore Cunningham. Wood trim, closets, and cabinetry reflect excellent carpentry. During remodeling, the current owners found unopened beer jugs behind walls of lathe and plaster from the Prohibition era. Below, Roger M. Davidson of Butte, Montana, built this house at 1205 Warm Springs Avenue with a matching garage to the rear for $15,000. Granite Hall is a spacious residence with a first floor of granite from a quarry owned by the architect, W. S. Campbell. The building features 15 rooms with geothermal heating. The backyard is connected via terraces to a canal that irrigates several properties. (Both PAP.)

Tourtellotte and Company designed this grand sandstone-and-frame Queen Anne house at 1409 Harrison Boulevard for Harry Wyman, a founder of Idaho Power. Finished in 1908, it features a terraced lot, front yard sunken pool, backyard fountains, and a Japanese hedge extending to Seventeenth Street. Anne Wyman called it the Rugosa after the pink-and-white flowering hedge. Even the small domed turret top has an Oriental appearance and admits light and air into the second story. The rear roofline is an ornamental ensemble lining resembling a miniature fence in Victorian architecture or the jagged geometric lines in the art deco style. The house's north end has a portico, a projecting porch whose roof or pediment is supported by a row of columns. This residence and surrounding landscape add to Boise's historic and current eclectic inventory of housing. (PAP.)

The Jordan-Wilcomb Construction Company built the recessed brick home above with Swiss-looking eaves and corners at 1002 Harrison Boulevard for Walter Dufresne. Touches of stucco are especially attractive on this residence, which may have been the first with a Tudor Revival design on the boulevard. As a new residence, it sold for $10,000 in 1925. J. Cecil Jordan constructed the impressive residence below at 1020 Harrison Boulevard in 1936. The family resided here for 20 years before Bank of Idaho president Joseph Bianco purchased the property. Charles Stuart started extensive restoration work in 1972. The building's brick and wood exterior and low, shingled roof recalls an English cottage or a Colonial home. (Both PAP.)

John H. Myer paid $5,000 for the home (above) at 1304 Harrison Boulevard in 1901. A Tourtellotte and Company Queen Anne villa made of stone from Table Rock and pine from a Placerville mill, it was the second-oldest house on Harrison until fire destroyed the first home near Hill Road. E. T. "Al" Fisher commissioned the Tourtellotte and Hummel Colonial Revival home below in 1941. The owner of a gold dredge at Warren in central Idaho, Fisher sold the house and his mining interests to potato king J. R. Simplot in 1946. The two-story framed building at 1500 Harrison Boulevard boasts an entryway with a circular porch, leaded glass, columns, an enclosed garden, and a sunroom built into a wall. (Both PAP.)

The striking California Mission–style house at 1505 Harrison Boulevard above was designed by Tourtellotte and Hummel and built for San Diego businessman G. W. Bond in 1911. The building was cast in reinforced concrete, a construction technique popularized by the San Francisco earthquake of 1906. The house featured a basement swimming pool covered as a dance floor. The cement lions were added later. Idaho governor David Davis once lived here. The stunning Queen Anne home below, at 1403 North Fifteenth Street, may have been designed by Tourtellotte and Company and was constructed in 1903 for sheep rancher Robert Butts in a pasture behind John Myer's orchard. Before the home was remodeled, the master bedroom opened onto the back porch. Parlor and kitchen beveled-glass windows, a square tower, flared eaves, gables, and slanted ceilings complement the Victorian character of the style. (Both PAP.)

The imposing edifice above at 901 North Seventeenth Street is a pleasing blend of Queen Anne and rectangular early-20th-century features. The former can be seen in leaded glass and columnar features. It also exhibits traits of the bungalow style with its broad eaves and extended rafters. Altogether, this two-and-a-half-story home with its architectural features and complementary front-yard trees and other landscaping is described as an example of the eclectic style. Still standing, the distinctive Craftsman-style residence at 924 West Fort Street below was built in 1901 for Hugh McElroy, a nine-year resident and the 35th attorney to be issued a license to practice law in the state of Idaho. Chinese vendors from Garden City parked their carts out front and sold fresh vegetables in the shade of a large black walnut tree. The home later housed nuns for St. John's Cathedral. (Both PAP.)

Milton D. Polk, president of Owyhee Land and Irrigation Company, bought the home above at 910 North Seventeenth Street when it was completed in 1910. It boasts a sandstone wraparound half-porch as well as half-timbers and stucco in its exterior. Such large bungalow-style residences, prized for their comfort and spaciousness, were popular among families with several children and are still enjoyed today in Boise's North End. What resembles a large box with rectangular corners and a diamond-shaped second-story decorative window at 809 North Eighteenth Street (below) was built in 1910. It represents a blending of Queen Anne characteristics with the design popular in that period. The front porch spans the facade with a portico, railing, and several columns. The leaded glass in the exterior was also a desirable feature, and vaulted ceilings were favored in the interior. (Both PAP.)

Bavarian-born Moses Alexander, left, and his Saxon wife, Helena, arrived in mid-July 1891 in Boise, where he started up a clothing store and became involved in the community. Alexander became widely known as "the One-Priced Clothier." In 1897, he was elected mayor for the first of two terms, and he later became the nation's first Jewish governor. In 1897, the year he was elected mayor, Moses Alexander also built the Queen Anne-style home below at 304 West State Street for his family. Its exterior once featured contrasting colors that today are muted by a pastel exterior finish. (Above ISHP; below PAP.)

Four

OUT AND ABOUT:
LIVING AND WORKING IN OLD BOISE

Boise has always been a place of accommodation for weary travelers and wanderers. Most could readily find a place of repose, whether it was a tough trail hand looking for a fistfight and a drink in a bar or a troubled seeker of solace and prayer in a local house of worship.

In the late 19th century and later, Boise featured two entirely different populations by day and by night. Ministers commented on the disparity of these two segments of society that seldom, if ever, came into contact with each other. The more refined elements of society, about whom much has been written, are often depicted and described in great detail, while the much larger working-class population and bar patrons have gone unrecognized.

Despite popular and populist merchants such as brewer John Lemp, who gave away a lot of lager beer and provided substance to the notion of a democratic governing class, Boise's moguls and mavens worked and shopped by day and entertained each other at night, far away from the downtown throngs.

The city's populace constantly shifted, but tradition and common heritage united most residents in their churchgoing as well as socializing habits and activities. This was a flourishing environment for merchants and peddlers of all sorts of goods, and Boiseans in the main were family-oriented, loved parades and concerts, and often took to the streets, if only for a stroll or to buy cigars or buttered popcorn from a vendor.

City transport evolved rapidly, from the paving of Main Street in 1897 and the trolley system that began in the 1890s to the passing popularity of bicycles and the appearance of the privately owned automobile, which began to dominate within a generation from 1910 to 1930. Boise even boasted a Ford assembly plant that helped kill the trolley system, the greatest tragedy for Boise and the surrounding valley. In 1908, a $100,000 bond to extend a greenbelt east of Julia Davis Park failed, and Boise still is attempting to undue past mistakes and pay for needed infrastructure improvements.

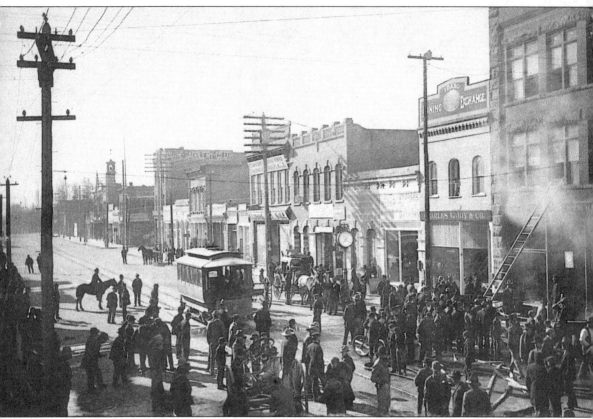

This photograph of streetcar No. 2 was taken on Main Street during the Coffin-Northrop Hardware Company fire on April 19, 1899. The Boise Valley Interurban electric railway trolley system began operations in 1891 and provided access to the brand-new natatorium at the east end of Warm Springs Avenue. Crews extended lines to Meridian in 1908 and to Caldwell in 1912, making a complete loop of the valley over 66 miles of track on both sides of the Boise River. Interurban cars carried freight, produce, milk cans, and bicycles as well as people from one end of the valley to the other. In 1904, a rival company, Boise Valley Railway, built a trolley line on the south side of the river from Boise to Caldwell that traversed Fairview Hill and continued on Ustick Road to principal stops in Meridian, Nampa, and Caldwell.

This *c.* 1915 photograph shows three streetcars stopped at the corner of Eighth and Bannock Streets in front of the Borah Post Office. The Interurban depot is to the left. By 1910, three trolley companies were operating, but they merged in 1912 as the Idaho Traction Company and in 1916 were acquired by Idaho Power Company. The trolley system connected people and places in the valley and shortened travel times, regardless of the weather. Boise residents could visit relatives in Star or attend events in Canyon County. The Canyon County Fair promoted "Boise Day" with special cars and fares to carry fairgoers from Boise. In 1909, over 5,000 people traveled to Canyon County on streetcars loaded to capacity. The trolley era ended abruptly in 1928, when the oil and automobile interests forced electric systems all over the U.S. into bankruptcy.

NATATORIUM, BOISE, IDAHO.

H. B. Eastman brought John Paulsen from Helena, Montana, to Boise in 1891 to design a natatorium for the geothermal water company. The "Nat," as it was known locally, was built in 1892 near the end of Warm Springs Avenue at the east end of a large homestead once owned by George Whitfield Russell. It featured geothermal hot water in its giant swimming pool and boasted twin six-story towers that incorporated elements of Moorish architecture surrounded by trees and lawns for outdoor picnics. The Nat quickly became a well-patronized recreational and social center and the most popular stop along the interurban loop for visitors of both sexes and all ages. The electric streetcars, noiseless save for the sound of wheels on rails, began their routes at the east end of Warm Springs Avenue in 1891 and spurred development of the natatorium.

For several decades, the natatorium on Warm Springs Avenue was a destination stop for visitors from all around the Boise Valley who planned their weekend outings and excursions to culminate in the recreational activities offered by this unparalleled area resource. Arched beams held up the vast interior of the natatorium, lending it the eerie look of a giant cavern or a railroad station. However, this aspect was softened somewhat by hanging plants and a second-story balcony with a railing from which intrepid swimmers slid all the way into the main pool area. What looks like a giant stone fireplace adorns one end. The Nat was an irreplaceable area social destination, and its likes have not been seen in the City of Trees before or since. The massive structure was severely damaged by a windstorm in 1934 and unfortunately was torn down.

The proprietor of this shoe shop is unknown but appears to be around 40 years of age posing outside his modest business, which specialized in the repair of footwear. The sandwich board sign at the left reads, "Repairing second hand shoes for sale." Cobblers were an important if undistinguished segment of the artisan population, and this photograph from around 1920 illustrates the humble conditions in which many of them worked. The photograph below of the Boise Rod and Gun Club was shot on Independence Day in 1900. Attendees were dressed up and wore hats and suspenders as they engaged in target practice. The presence of young boys interspersed behind the line of shooters suggest this was a father-son event, and all of them traveled to the site, which was probably south of the Boise River, in horse-drawn buggies or on bicycles. (Both ISHS.)

In the undated post-1900 photograph above, a horse-drawn carriage parked on Ninth Street between Idaho and Main Streets has been converted to a street-vending vehicle from which its proprietors sold fresh roasted peanuts and buttered popcorn for 5¢ a bag. Note the elaborate features, including wrought-iron frontispieces, and more common touches, such as the bucket behind the right front wheel and the wooden stops holding all the wheels in place. Note also the bicycles on the sidewalk. Below, A. G. Thompson's two-story wood-frame Wagon Shop was photographed in 1891, when the local business at 823 Eighth Street appeared in the city directory. Thompson and his two-man crew specialized in building, painting, and repairing carriages and wagons. From the lumber scraps and wheel fragments evident in the photograph, this was a popular and busy place where local residents took their conveyances for touch up and repair. (Both ISHS.)

The 1900 photograph above shows 10 apple pickers in Abbott's Orchard near the Belfry School on Five Mile Road north of Ustick Road. Railroad transport in the late 1880s galvanized the fruit industry, and soon large growers such as Thomas Davis were shipping carloads of applies, prunes, and agricultural products to Montana and other destinations. Surveyor general Lafayette Cartee and others grew nurseries that truly made Boise a city of trees. Until the 1960s, the original state fair held every late summer in Boise was sited south of Fairview Avenue and west of Orchard Street, where the I-84 connector now runs. The 1915 photograph below shows a large-scale barbeque and hundreds of famished fairgoers eagerly awaiting service by dozens of volunteers. Carnival rides, games, and livestock shows were also important components of this annual event. (Both ISHS.)

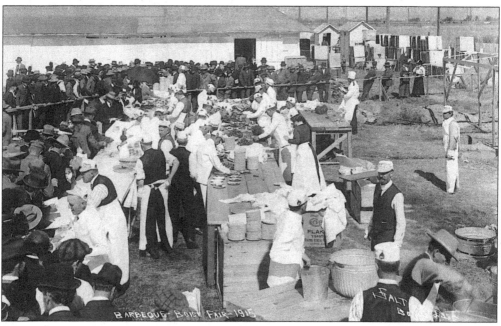

Above, the restored city-owned depot on the south end of Capitol Boulevard is the site of numerous festivals and weddings and still serves as a depot during rare train stops. Below, the New York architectural firm of Carrere and Hastings built the Union Pacific depot in 1925 on the bench overlooking downtown, serving the first mainline train into Boise. The southwest Mission-style building is a local landmark with a white clock-and-bell tower. It replaced two earlier downtown stations between Ninth and Tenth Streets, a wooden structure and another of sandstone blocks. (Above LC; below J. McGee/IP.)

West German native John Lemp (left) moved to Boise in 1864 at age 26. He built a brewery and in 1868 reportedly bought another from Peter Sturtzenacher for a teacup filled with gold dust. By 1873, he had a Main Street storehouse and produced more beer than anyone else in Idaho Territory. He became Boise's first German-born mayor in 1875. Charles F. Hummel designed the Turnverein Building (below) at 100 South Fifth Street. The German athletic club held its inaugural on March 22, 1870. Until sold in 1916, the building hosted dances and sporting events for the 711 Germans recorded in the 1910 census. (Both ISHS.)

Popular Boise saloon keeper and lifelong Democrat James Hinmond Hart (right) was born on May 23, 1834, in New York City, where he was as an apprentice and typesetter for the *New York Times*. He journeyed to San Francisco and Orofino before 1862 found him in the Boise Basin, where peddling liquor paid more than mining. He operated bars southwest of Placerville, in Helena, Montana, and on Main Street in Boise. Eliza Paynton (below) married James Hart in November 1866 in New York City. They had seven children, including James Jr., born in 1873. In 1871, the family traveled by rail to Kelton, Utah, then by stagecoach through Boise and on to Placerville but moved to Boise in 1871. (Both ISHS.)

The photograph above of Lawrence and Smith's Saloon from 1890 shows the liquors and cigars available. Saloon keeper Richard Adelmann worked in his business while investing and working mining properties. Main Street saloon keeper James K. Lawrence served a clientele consisting of respectable and sober patrons as well as beggars and drunkards. Below, the Jellison brothers of Boise established their successful retail monument business in 1917 at 510 Main Street, where tombstones were produced for sale until the early 1970s. The wrought-iron fence below is part of an elaborate outdoor display of the polished, finished sandstone markers carved locally from the "finest rainbow granites." (Above ISHS; below OBHD.)

On the right is Walter E. Pierce, Boise's most prolific real estate promoter from 1890 until 1930, who pioneered the use of large display advertisements in daily newspapers to maximize exposure of new subdivisions and houses. He had a habit of reserving an elegant residence for himself in each new project that he later sold at a handsome profit. In 1914, he built the Governor's Mansion at 1905 North Twenty-first Street. He and his partners, L. H. Cox and John M. Haines, greatly impacted Boise's residential and commercial appearance. Below, Pierce Park on the interurban loop was a popular swimming and boating attraction in 1910. (Both ISHS.)

Pierce Park, Boise, Idaho

Above, the horse-drawn carriage with comfortable button-and-tufted upholstered seats and spring axles was a standard mode of local transportation and especially warm-weather outings until the advent of the automobile after 1910. Below, the horse-drawn sleigh enabled Boiseans to traverse deep snow drifts in winter before the coming of paved roadways. (Both PAP/OBHD.)

Above, this distinctive "ice wagon" at 1311 Warm Springs Avenue is an authentic single-person carriage that was extremely popular in downtown Boise at the end of the 19th century. Its owners, Allyn and Philip Krueger, found it on the highway to Weiser and returned it to their East Boise home. It has been used as a Wells Fargo wagon in local musicals and is adorned during the holiday season with a large "Toys" sign on its side. Below, children's tricycles were found in affluent neighborhoods including Warm Springs Avenue, Harrison Boulevard, and the North End, where sidewalks prevailed. (Above PAP; below PAP/OBHD.)

Hannifin's Cigar Store at 1024 West Main Street, across from the Owyhee Hotel, was built in 1908, but no historic photographs are known to exist. The tobacconist enjoyed a status in the society and the economy of the 19th-century frontier town comparable to the saloon keeper and haberdasher. Then as now, downtown pedestrians frequent these establishments for reasons of interaction as well as taste. Today's shop features restored signage. The undated photograph below of a farmer's market in Boise was probably taken during the Great Depression and depicts an older man in overalls straightening a sack of produce among bushel baskets of apples and other commodities. This commercial operation is conducted from the back of a truck with wooden boards and slats on three sides. (Above PAP; below LC.)

This 1895 photograph (above) shows Christ Chapel, a white frame Gothic Revival building known as St. Michael's Episcopal Church when constructed in 1866. It now occupies Boise State University's northeast corner, where the Boise River meets the Broadway Bridge. After the Civil War, Gothic replaced Greek Revival as a dominant U.S. architectural style. The photograph to the right of the First Baptist Church was taken around 1900. Thirty-four years earlier, its first incarnation was the second church building in the territorial capital. The first two Baptist churches stood on the northwest corner of Ninth and Idaho Streets. The current church sits on the west side of Thirteenth Street at 607 North Thirteenth across from Boise High School. (Both ISHS.)

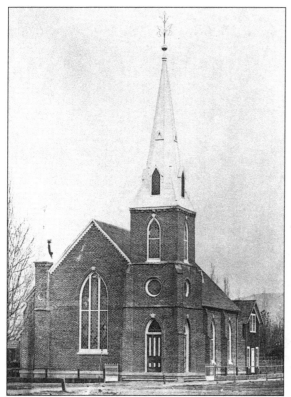

The original First Methodist Church (at left) was a brick building constructed in 1874 at Eighth and Bannock Streets, but it was torn down to make room for Hotel Boise. This is the first brick church in Boise; its design was Gothic Revival and featured a tall tower. The second First Methodist Church (below) was built in 1906. Some of its features resemble Greek Orthodox, with a large tall and imposing multi-layer rectangular column that appeared increasingly Byzantine the further up it went. The even more spectacular and larger current church at 717 North Eleventh Street is called the Cathedral of the Rockies and was built in the 1960. (Both ISHS.)

The site of the original First United Presbyterian Church (at right), the northeast of corner of Main and Tenth Streets, is now occupied by the Idanha Hotel. Some early furnishings brought to Boise in covered wagons in 1878 were relocated with the church to Tenth and State Streets. Today's building began in 1929 with an education center, a sanctuary followed in 1954 and Lindsay Hall at Ninth and State Streets was added in 1967. Beth Israel Synagogue (below) was completed in 1895 at 1102 West State Street. The oldest synagogue west of the Mississippi still in use by the original congregation has a century-old organ and geometric stained-glass windows. Synagogue organizers were David Falk and the first Jewish governor in the United States, Moses Alexander. The building was recently relocated to a new campus immediately south of Morris Hill Cemetery. (Both ISHS.)

Catholics played an important role in the evolution of Boise's Christian community. The first mass was conducted in John O'Farrell's cabin in 1863, and successive churches tell a story of increasing style and importance and of rebounding from disaster with a firm faith in the future. Boise's first Catholic church building burned to the ground 18 days after it was finished in 1870. A second frame building, above, was constructed at Ninth and Bannock Streets in 1876. The current cathedral, St. John's, below, was designed by Tourtellotte and Hummel and dedicated in 1921 at 804 North Eighth Street. The Romanesque Revival sandstone structure has vaulted ceilings, marble floors, and stained-glass windows. Altars, statues, and oil paintings on canvas adorn the interior. A large Tudor-style residence behind the cathedral is the rectory and dates from 1905. (Both ISHS.)

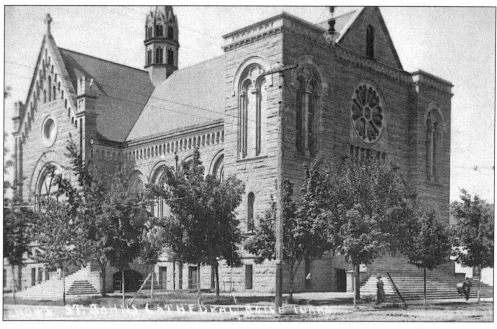

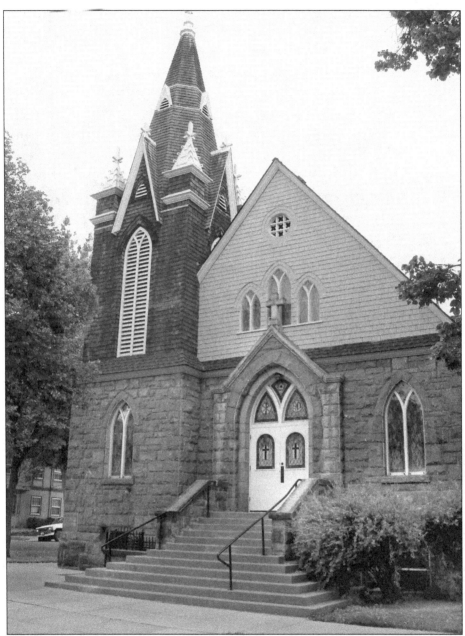

Immanuel Lutheran Church at Seventh and Fort Streets began as the Swedish Lutheran Church of the Augustana Synod, which was designed by Charles Hummel and is on the National Register of Historic Buildings. This Gothic Revival building is of local rusticated sandstone. In 1906, Rev. Charles Bengston of Idaho Falls organized the congregation with 19 Swedish-speaking Scandinavian charter members. Officials paid $3,500 for the site and broke ground on May 26, 1908. The building was finished during the pastorate of Rev. C. C. Olsson and dedicated on September 22, 1915. On October 1, 1918, all services were held in English, and the doors opened to all Boise Lutherans. The name was changed in 1919 to Evangelical Lutheran Immanuel Church. By the late 1950s, the original building was named Augustana Chapel to recognize its original synodical affiliation and to distinguish it from the more modern structure. (PAP.)

A Tuscan portico dominates the entryway of the Church of Jesus Christ of Latter-day Saints tabernacle constructed in 1924 at 900 West Washington Street. The building itself is in the Colonial style, popular in that era, with large rectangular eaves extending from two rooflines and a round porthole window in between the rooflines. Later Mormon churches, including the large temple built from 1982 until 1984, are distinguished by more modern architectural styles with a needle-like spire on top. Mormons contributed greatly to community building in southern Idaho, and Bishop James H. Hart served in the territorial legislature. They endured discrimination, supported funding of the state capitol in the 1880s, and later fought efforts to repeal federal and state prohibition of liquor sales. This helped the anti-saloon traditionalists prevent the private sale of hard liquor and led Idaho into the state liquor sales business.

Five

TRIAL AND PUNISHMENT

On December 30, 1905, former governor Frank Steunenberg opened his garden gate in Caldwell, triggering a bomb explosion that claimed his life an hour later. The assassin, Canadian-born Harry Orchard, had walked nearly a mile back to the Saratoga Hotel where he was staying when the blast occurred. He was no doubt smiling when he entered the bar, found the bartender alone, and called for a drink. He was arrested and brought to trial against Western Federation of Miners boss "Big Bill" Haywood on May 10, 1907. Special prosecutors James Hawley and newly elected U.S. senator William Borah prepared to square off against a defense team led by famed attorney Clarence Darrow. It took three weeks to select a jury of 12 farmers and ranchers, many from Meridian, from the pool of 248 prospective jurors. By the end of the 10-week trial, Darrow had convinced the jury that Orchard possibly acted out of revenge against Steunenberg, and not in the employ of the union. Darrow secured an acquittal for Haywood, and Orchard was eventually sentenced to death. That was commuted to life in prison, and the confessed assassin spent most of the next half-century inside the dank granite walls of the Idaho State Penitentiary. Haywood later fled to Soviet Russia, where he died in 1929 and was buried in the Kremlin.

As a convict, Orchard underwent a startling conversion to the same Seventh-day Adventist faith as the former governor. His victim's widow forgave her husband's murderer, a self-confessed violent anarchist, wife-stealer, card cheat, and general con artist, in a public statement. Celebrated actress Ethel Barrymore, who attended a session of the trial, also visited Orchard in prison. For the next several decades, Orchard was a model prisoner who spent his last years as a trustee on the prison chicken farm, where he became quite an expert on poultry raising and diseases. He became almost synonymous with the massive and medieval-looking institution on the north side of Warm Springs Boulevard under the shadow-casting foothills crest of Table Rock. Offered a pardon, he declined and died in prison in 1956.

This statue of former governor Frank Steunenberg faces the state capitol from the south side of Jefferson Street. The inscription reads, "Frank Steunenberg, Governor of Idaho, 1887–1900. When in 1899 organized lawlessness challenged the power of Idaho, he upheld the dignity of the state, enforced its authority and restored law and order within its boundaries, for which he was assassinated in 1905. 'Rugged in body, resolute in mind, massive in the strength of his convictions, he was of the granite-hewn.' In grateful memory of his courageous devotion to public duty, the people of Idaho have erected this monument." Steunenberg was fatally injured by a bomb planted on his garden gate in Caldwell by an alleged agent of the Western Federation of Miners, who resented the former chief executive for calling in troops to quell labor unrest in northern Idaho. (PAP.)

Defendant Harry Orchard (1) is on the witness stand at left in the Ada County Courthouse on June 13, 1907. The others, in numerical order, are (2) John Murphy, Western Federation of Miners attorney; (3) William Miner, Bill Haywood's father-in-law; (4) Henrietta Haywood, Bill's youngest daughter; (5) Vernie Haywood, his eldest daughter; (6) Mary Carruthers, his half-sister; (7) Leon Whitsell; (8) Peter Breen; (9) Clarence Darrow; (10) Etta Carruthers, Haywood's mother; (11) William D. Haywood; (12) John F. Nugent; (13) Edmund F. Richardson; (14) Harry Crane; and (15) Martin Egan and (16) William Kennedy of the Associated Press. Not pictured are prosecuting attorneys James H. Hawley, a later governor, and William E. Borah, a later U.S. senator who earned a national and even international reputation as the "Lion of Idaho," a great orator who did not favor America's entry into World War I.

From left to right, George Pettibone, Bill Haywood, and Charles Moyer were accused of ordering Harry Orchard to murder former governor Steunenberg. All leaders of the Western Federation of Miners, they stood trial separately. Prosecutors first tried Haywood, because he was considered more vulnerable due to blindness in one eye and a tendency to lose his temper, contrasted to the more cooperative appearance of Moyer and Pettibone. The state was appealing to the jury, because its investigator had been unable to corroborate the confession of Orchard, who also admitted to killing 16 other people. But the jury was not swayed by Orchard, who claimed he had converted after the state provided him with a small library of religious booklets. Haywood and Pettibone were acquitted, the latter after the defense declined to argue the case, and the charges against Moyer were dropped.

The star witness for the prosecution in the Haywood trial of 1907, Harry Orchard, confessed to over 20 crimes, including murdering enemies of the Western Federation of Miners. He spent the rest of his life in the penitentiary, where in January 1909 he was baptized into the Seventh-day Adventist Church in the so-called plunge bath. The photograph below was taken on June 15, 1907, and shows witness Orchard with guards and detectives during transport. From left to right are warden E. L. Whitney, Colorado state's witness Deputy Bartell, Orchard, penitentiary guard Daniel Ackley, E. D. Hawley, and famed Pinkerton Agency detective Charles Siringo. Not identified is the dapper yet somber driver sporting gloves and a fine bowler. (Both ISHS.)

This photograph of attorney William Edgar Borah was taken near the end of his distinguished six-term U.S. Senate career and is inscribed to a local colleague, George L. Ambrose, a police judge (also known as a magistrate) in Meridian. Borah arrived in Boise in late 1890 from Illinois and Kansas and was the keynote speaker at the July Fourth festivities in 1891. By 1892, he was chairman of the Republican state party, and four years later, he lost his first bid as a candidate for Congress. In 1907, he served as special prosecutor in the sensational trial of Haywood and other labor union bosses. Borah as senator was known as the "Lion of Idaho" and an isolationist in foreign affairs after World War I, but he fought long and hard for diplomatic recognition of the Soviet Union by the United States. (PAP.)

The plaque above commemorates the founding of Idaho's principal penal institution one mile east of downtown Boise at the foot of Table Rock, which was used as a lookout by Shoshone natives. Lewiston and Boise fought fiercely over the site of the prison, and this bitter regional rivalry delayed plans presented to the territorial legislature. The U.S. Department of the Interior ruled in favor of Boise. Convicts quarried sandstone from the Table Rock area to build the fortress-like territorial prison. Construction began in 1868, and in 1893–1894, inmates built the sandstone wall that still surrounds the compound and which measures 17 feet in height and 2.5 feet in width. Stone buttresses support the wall's exterior; pipe railing and planks form a catwalk along which guards stationed in the turret-like tower patrolled the yard. (Both PAP.)

In 1894, workers finished the administration building, 22 years after the prison opened. Horse-drawn wagons carried supplies and quarried stones through a tunnel into the yard. The warden's office and other offices were here, with the library, dispensary, deputy warden's sleeping quarters, and guards' reading room on the first floor. Sleeping quarters for single guards were on the second floor, while the southwest corner tower housed the armory. The grounds of the Old Penitentiary featured natural beauty with flourishing rose bushes and meticulously maintained grounds. Accompanying this was a sense of terror instilled by the massive sandstone walls and reinforced by inmate-designed cylindrical towers on the corners of the main yard's wall. (Both PAP.)

This photograph depicts the north wing of a main cell block. On the second of four tiers, the characters "# 4–Nikolay 1885" can still be seen clearly. The old Territorial Prison in 1872 accommodated 39 men; in 1878, it held 90 men and one woman. After the administration building was constructed in 1893–1894 by convicts serving hard time for murder, robbery, and selling liquor to Indians, the penitentiary had expanded capacity. It housed 13,000 convicts over 100 years, including 215 women. The maximum number held at one time was 603. The previous arrangement of solitary confinement and isolation, known as the Pennsylvania system, was replaced by the 1870s by the congregate or Auburn system. Inmates were permitted to eat and work as a group and were confined to tiny sleeping cells at night. The authorities encouraged silence but not complete isolation. (PAP.)

DEATH ROW

A prisoner sentenced to death occupied a cell on Death Row while awaiting his execution date.

The only man to be hanged on the adjoining gallows spent a ... Death Row in 1957.

GALLOWS TRAP DOOR WEIGHT AND STOP

There were only 10 executions at the Idaho State Penitentiary, which was closed in 1973 after violent riots and the near destruction of several buildings. All 10 death-row residents were hanged for murder, including Raymond Snowden, convicted of the murder of Cora Dean and hanged in the gallows of 5 House in 1957. Visitors to the Old Pen, a tourist attraction and administrative division of the Idaho Historical Society, walk from the second-floor death row downstairs to the gallows trap door on the ground floor. Still visible are the weight and pulley mechanisms by which a prisoner's neck was snapped in execution of his sentence. (Both PAP.)

Early wardens resided in a small wood-frame house outside the walls. In 1894, warden J. P. Campbell moved his family onto the second floor of the new administration building, while still using their former house as a kitchen and dining room. In 1901, John Tourtellotte drew the plans for the warden's house, which was finished the next year. In 1954, a new warden's house was completed. A colorful array of characters served as warden, especially around the beginning of the 20th century. Warden Charles Van Dorn was arrested in 1899 for beating a guard, Douglas Hix, with a set of large keys. Van Dorn had accused Hix of negligence; the latter called the warden a liar, and an argument erupted. The warden beat the guard unconscious and later pled guilty to a misdemeanor, paid a fine of $20, and resigned. (PAP.)

Above, in 1902, when inmate Josie Kensler became pregnant, a ward for women was necessary. Kensler accused warden Charles Arney and the prison doctor of inducing an abortion. Public outrage forced Arney's resignation and spurred calls for a separate women's ward. Unlike male convicts, women cooked their own meals and sewed their own clothing in the seven two-person cells. Over its 48-year history, the women's ward sheltered 214 women; half a dozen escaped. Kensler was released in 1909 for good behavior. In the image below, the warden's previous residence was made available in 1906. Workers enclosed the area with a wall. In 1920, a new women's ward dormitory was finished with a capacity for 14 women. Between 1908 and 1947, nine women served time for adultery. (Both PAP.)

Six

EDUCATION AND
MEDICINE

The first private school in Boise consisted of a group of frontier pupils taught by F. B. Smith in a log cabin in the winter of 1863–1864. Other private schools emerged, but most were of short duration. Progress toward an organized public school system, let alone a modern medical facility complex, was painfully slow. Boise's coming of age waited until the decades after 1900, when educational and medical institutions in the form of schools, libraries, and hospitals developed through long years of struggle.

The population tripled between 1900 and 1920, when a public school system was in place and several hospitals provided needed medical services. In 1932, Boise Junior College was founded and functioned for seven years as a nonprofit corporation inside St. Margaret's School at First and Idaho Streets. It was moved in 1938 to its current location at one end of the runway at Boise Municipal Airport.

Today, Boise State University (BSU), the city's public library and school systems, and two state-of-the-art medical centers, St. Luke's and Saint Alphonsus, embody the excellence earned through many decades of hard work and determination.

The first schoolhouse in Boise was built in 1868 on the site of the Carnegie-funded first public library on the southwest corner of Washington and North Eighth Streets. The brick building was a former carriage painting shop and housed three teachers in tiny rooms so cramped that pupils were forced to attend in half-day shifts. One can only imagine how challenging such frontier conditions were to teachers and pupils, including heating in winter as well ventilation in summer and plumbing. Such buildings had only a wood or coal stove for heating and no running water, and students were crowded together, making the learning process very difficult indeed. The juxtaposition of the old and the new, as depicted in this 1905 photograph where the scaffolding on the library building is evident, could not be more striking.

The 1883 Central School was one of several large brick public buildings constructed in the 1880s, along with the Ada County Courthouse in 1881 and the Territorial Capitol in 1886. On February 4, 1881, the territorial legislature by special charter created the Independent School District of Boise City. The charter authorized the sale of bonds to build a school to be completed by September 1882 and to open as "a union graded free school." This four-story, 16-classroom building and its brick-and-mortar neighbors occupied a former sagebrush area designated for public buildings in the 1860s. A mansard roof and a cupola characterized the school. Organizers were severely criticized for the building's enormous size, but by 1894, Central School was overrun with students, making necessary the construction of additional buildings in the later 1890s and early 20th century.

Hawthorne School (above) began as a two-room frame building near the famed natatorium. In 1900, it was removed, and another was partially built prior to annexation into the Boise District in 1907. This building was vacated in 1932, when the land reverted to the Coston estate. In 1951, fourteen barracks-style classrooms were built along Targee Street. In 1955, officials drew up plans for an 18-classroom permanent structure, but limited funds allowed only a 5-room facility, and Hawthorne was not completely finished until 1961. The old Garfield School (below) was annexed by the Boise District in 1910 and was used until 1950. (Both ISHS.)

The Little Tutor Shop served scores of pupils as a kindergarten in Yeoman Apartments, or Yeoman Flats as printed in the city directory. The large rectangular building was constructed of sandstone blocks and featured a columned entryway. In the early years of the 20th century, the institution was under the management of Julia Capwell, who was an experienced teacher in the Boise public school system. Prior to accepting a position with the Yeoman Apartments, she served as the kindergarten teacher at St. Margaret's Academy. The photograph above was taken around 1918 and shows many ornately dressed young misses among 14 young scholars in their finest apparel. One of them poses with his left foot on the wooden board of a scooter and another, decked out in a sailor suit, proudly poses with an American flag over his shoulder.

The Boise High School football team in the autumn of 1909 consisted of a 10-man squad and coach. Note the shin guards and the jovial atmosphere generated by team members' apparent camaraderie. In the background at the far left is a younger male student, possibly a younger brother of a team member. Boise High School, at 1010 Washington Street, is a neoclassical Grecian building. The "plant" was begun with the east wing in 1908, followed by the west wing in 1912. The Industrial Arts Building was erected in 1920 across the street, and the center section of the main plant replaced the original structure in 1922. A 1936 gymnasium replaced the basement facility, and band and chorus rooms were added in 1961. (Both ISHS.)

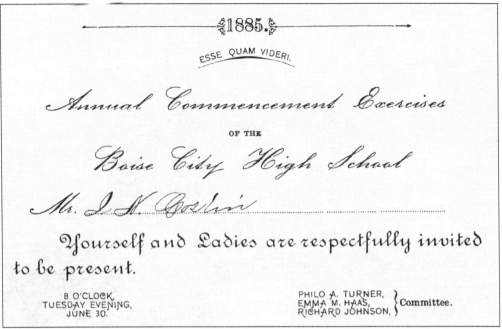

ESSE QUAM VIDERI.

Annual Commencement Exercises

OF THE

Boise City High School

Mr. I. N. Coston

Yourself and Ladies are respectfully invited to be present.

8 O'CLOCK,
TUESDAY EVENING,
JUNE 30.

PHILO A. TURNER, }
EMMA M. HAAS, } Committee.
RICHARD JOHNSON, }

An invitation to attend the annual commencement exercises at Boise City High School on June 30, 1885, is pictured above. Link's Modern Business College was once called the "Best Commercial School in the West." The 1910 photograph below by M. D. Martin depicts adults learning phonograph operation, typewriting, and dictation using earphones. The three young men probably reflected the ratio of male to female graduates. Hanging at the rear of the room is a framed photograph of a woman with proper posture engaged in practicing typewriting. The school was later known as Link's School of Business until its metamorphosis into ITT Tech. (Above PLS; below ISHS.)

In June 1902, Mary C. (Mrs. James) Beatty sent a letter through her husband, a judge, to Andrew Carnegie that resulted in a $25,000 grant for the city's first library, which had been operating and expanding in city hall since mid-February 1894. Mrs. Beatty was president of the library board appointed by Mayor Moses Alexander in 1903, when it was learned that Carnegie would deal only with cities, not clubs. The city was required to furnish a site, keep an annual maintenance fund equal to 10 percent of the grant, and furnish population and pro-library statistics. The site was obtained from the school district, and voters approved a half-mill library tax levy. The Carnegie Library Building at 815 West Washington Street, built in 1904–1905 with a brick exterior and sandstone trim and interior features of woodwork and polished marble, was one of Tourtellotte and Company's finest in the Renaissance Revival style.

In June 1895, Ella Cartee Reed, a daughter of surveyor general Lafayette Cartee, took charge of Boise's first library, housed inside city hall and established in 1894 by the Columbian Club. The first paid librarian served for nine years and built the holdings from 832 books for $20 a month. Below, Mary Wood, Boise's librarian from 1903 to 1913, was the last to oversee the library inside city hall and the first to serve in the new Carnegie Library. In 1904, the City Hall Library had 6,000 books and 24,000 visitors. Wood resigned to become the wife of Elmer J. Smith of Detroit. (Both ISHS.)

Ella Cartée Reed

St. Luke's Hospital began in 1902, when the Episcopal Church established a 10-bed medical facility in a home at 190 East Bannock Street. Expansions occurred in 1928 and 1977, when the hospital boasted 300 beds and a 24-hour emergency department. It offers cancer treatment, cardiac care, pediatrics, and maternal and childcare. The undated photograph below shows two well-dressed older gentlemen wearing derby hats and suits around the horse-drawn St. Luke's Hospital private ambulance. The hospital first opened in 1902, before the arrival of automobiles. The vents at the top of the wagon probably relate to ventilation rather than heating. (Both ISHS.)

Saint Alphonsus Hospital opened on December 27, 1894, on the site of the earliest Catholic church in Boise. Bishop A. J. Glorieux obtained an advance of $25,000 from a Catholic order in Indiana to build the facility. In 1902, the hospital expanded from a small facility of 25 beds with a staff of four to a larger complex more suited to a municipality. Scotsman William Stewart Campbell designed this facility as well as the Idanha Hotel in the same style of French chateau architecture. His firm was taken over by his partner, Charles Wayland, who came to Boise in 1900 and worked as a draftsman in Campbell's office before becoming a partner in 1902. Part of the original Saint Alphonsus complex still stands on the east side of the State Office Tower, but the hospital itself expanded and relocated to I-84 and Curtis Road.

One of Boise's dominant architects in the 1890s was James King, who relocated in 1888 from Huntington, West Virginia. He designed several large buildings on Eighth Street in the downtown area and the structure named the Oddfellows Hall, finished in 1889. He also designed the chateau-style Idaho Soldiers' Home, pictured here, which burned in 1900. John Tourtellotte transformed the building into a Moorish-style palace with a central onion dome. King also designed the 1893 administration building at the Old Idaho Penitentiary, which is on the National Register of Historic Places. In 1891, King employed the French chateau style again for a brick mansion built for banker C. W. Moore at Warm Springs Avenue and Walnut Street. King also designed an Episcopal rectory at Idaho and Second Streets that later became the Bishop's House and a large stone and shingle house on Warm Springs Avenue.

On the right, Pres. Eugene Chaffee operates heavy equipment during the ground-breaking ceremony of Boise Junior College (BJC) at its current site on March 7, 1940. Below, Boise State University was originally founded in 1932 as Boise Junior College when the Episcopal Church Diocese of Idaho donated St. Margaret's School at First and Idaho Streets to the city. Until 1939, BJC was a nonprofit corporation supported by a group of Boise businessmen. In 1940, the college was moved to its present location at one end of the runway of Boise Municipal Airport after the Idaho Legislature established a taxing district for the junior college. (Both ISHS.)

Above, Boise State University's Administration Building was built in 1940 on the site of the former Boise Municipal Airport runway on the south side of the Boise River west of Broadway Avenue. The library below is today known as the Albertson Library. BSU's repository of hard-copy holdings and electronic library files has served a growing student population through the institution's various incarnations as Boise Junior College from 1932, Boise College from 1965, Boise State College from 1969, and the present Boise State University from 1974. BSU is now Idaho's largest institution of higher learning, with nearly 20,000 enrolled graduate and undergraduate students. (Both ISHS.)

Seven

CHINESE AND OTHER MINORITIES

In 1868, a census showed 1,134 permanent residents in Boise, excluding several hundred Shoshone Indians who were chased out of the area. In 1870, only 20 newcomers were African Americans, and over 100 Chinese were counted from the Eighth Street laundry district. By 1900, Ada County's census reported 536 non-whites among nearly 8,000 Europeans, with slightly over 2,000 listed as "foreign born." There were even 200 Japanese migrants in or near the city, but Hispanics and Basques who only spent the winter in town were difficult to tally and therefore were ignored. The numbers of white Boiseans included many of ethnic groups, such as Germans, Jews, Canadians, Dutchmen, and Irishmen.

Boise has always tended to keep its ethnic diversity well hidden, to the point that the U.S. Census in 2002 reported 93 percent of its residents were Caucasian, and only Livonia, Michigan, was a whiter medium-sized municipality. If the Native Americans who were driven from Boise and subjected to occasional shootings if they wandered back too close to the river experienced the stress of isolation, other minorities felt the unspoken sting of segregation. Traditionally Boise has spawned and supported more covert than overt racism; for example, there were no reports of lynching of blacks in the City of Trees. Published histories focus on whites' "firsts," such as Boise's first place of worship in an Irishman's log cabin.

There was a diminution of Native American success in fending off early white invaders and a subsequent minimizing or ridiculing of other non-white groups, who gravitated to the same blocks in a given area, forming ethnic enclaves or pockets of non-white residential and commercial activity. As the whites forced their old world and Midwest views of estate mansions and landscaped grounds on a desert plateau, the few minority representatives, including several Chinese businessmen who did well in this city from 1870 onward, prospered because of the resourcefulness and resilience they displayed in blending into white society.

The close-up above shows young Chinese males carrying a dragon and a lion near the corner of Seventh and Main Streets. Chinese were as enthusiastic about holidays and parades as whites and, until about 1910, dressed in their finest silk clothes, carried banners from their temples, and danced while Chinese bands played for the occasion. Below, a c. 1900 scene from the Chinese New Year also at Main and Seventh Streets suggest how important celebrations were to Boise's Chinese population. In the foreground at left, the Boise Business and Shorthand College at 105 South Seventh Street is visible. (Both ISHS.)

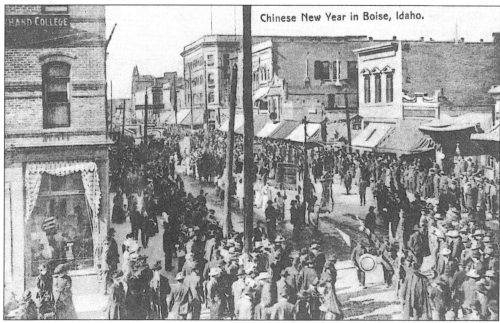

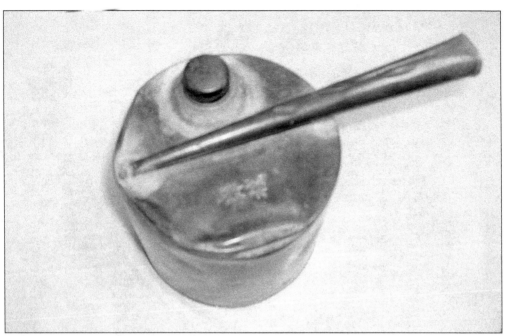

Chinese laundry workers in the late 19th century used this brass mister or atomizer to spray clothes with water during ironing. The utensil replaced an earlier technique of spraying water from the mouth, a habit that was denigrated by white laundrymen who said it was simply spitting on the clothes. Bits of Chinese pottery, intact or in shards, are still found today in remote mining regions of the Boise Basin 40 miles northeast of Boise. These small, hand-painted items of daily use are prized by collectors and were found in every Chinese household, including Boise's Chinatown district, from 1870 onward. (Both PW/PAP.)

Every culture associates feasting with celebration and a robust way of life. This 1897 photograph depicts a Chinese man interacting with two well-dressed white adults, one of them pointing to a whole roast pig, which was often found in the celebratory feasts, while the other looks on with both hands in his pockets. Note the cluster and clutter of lean-tos and containers that crowd the rear left of the photograph. The Chinese kept to themselves and displayed a dignity in friendship to whites that was not always reciprocated. They were always hospitable during their holiday celebrations and kept their best dainties and delicacies on hand for visitors and friends. In the 1920s, Chinese associations held banquets and invited many local white dignitaries. Hosts included the Fong, Louie, and Kwong family patriarchs, many of whom were members of the Chinese Masons.

Between 1901 and 1920, half a dozen Chinese eateries served bird's nest soup, chicken, fried spareribs with pineapple and bamboo sprouts, duck with mushrooms and chestnuts, and chop suey, which was invented in America. Harry Fong began his Boise career in 1923 as a cook in the Sunshine Café and later owned the Bamboo Garden Restaurant on Capitol Boulevard. In 1927, Harry retrieved an 18-year-old bride from a peasant village in Kwantung Province in China (below). "The first lady of Chinatown," Gretta helped run the restaurant and bore four children; the first-born son, Harry Jr., died in infancy. Gretta died in 1937. (Both ISHS.)

The gardener above worked for an affluent Boise family. When Chinese and blacks were restricted from mining in the 1870s, they resorted to gardening. The words "Chinese gardens" contracted to Chinden in naming the boulevard through Garden City supplying everyone with fresh produce. Gardeners walked or drove wagons and, later, Model T Ford trucks. They generated yields from small plots. Dr. C. K. Ah Fong (left) lived in Rocky Bar before moving to Boise in 1889. C. K. won a court battle over his right to be licensed by the State of Idaho as a physician and became the first Chinese doctor in Idaho. (Both ISHS.)

This *c.* 1910 photograph, entitled "Chinese Hank and Ham," shows the duo smoking opium pipes. The Chinese government forbade the opium industry, but in the two Opium Wars of 1839–1842 and 1856–1860, the Royal Navy forced the legalization of the opium trade. Much of what was consumed in America came from India. In 1879, the *Idaho Statesman* said over $7,000 worth of opium was smoked annually in Boise by Chinese and white males. This practice probably did more than anything else to generate anti-Chinese sentiment and led to the first razing of Chinese buildings in Boise, starting in 1901. Most violence was connected to consumption of alcohol, not opium, which induces euphoria and tranquility in its users. But most whites saw in the Chinese an inferior class of pestilential invaders who took jobs from Christians and deserved discrimination.

Although he was often assumed to be of Basque descent, Jesus Urquides was born in Sonora, Mexico, in 1833 and learned the mule-packing business in California before coming to Idaho Territory in the early 1860s. He established his mule-train headquarters in Boise's "Spanish Village" and made a very difficult living packing his mules with everything from food, clothing, and even machinery for the remote mining camps of the Boise Basin. A celebrated eccentric, he was often featured in parades as late as the 1920s. This 1925 photograph of Urquides in his 90s illustrates that he could still load and secure several large, heavy barrels on a mule's back. People today might object to this mistreatment of animals. Before his death, he commented that were he to start over, he would find an easier livelihood than mule-train packing. (UI.)

Cyrus Jacobs came to Boise by way of Iowa, the Oregon Trail, Portland, and Walla Walla. He started a pack train that freighted supplies from Walla Walla to Idaho City. In 1858, he married Mary Ellen Palmer in Oregon. Jacobs was a merchant, miller, meatpacker, and whiskey distiller of Jacobs' Best. The couple had six children; Cyrus was a city councilman elected mayor in 1880. Below, Jacobs family members stands in front of Boise's oldest surviving brick residence, built by Cyrus Jacobs in 1864, at 607 Grove Street, adjacent to the Basque Museum. It is listed on the National Register of Historic Places. (Both ISHS.)

On the left, an unidentified sheepherder is pictured with one of his charges. Immigrants from the Pyrenees settled in California and Nevada before relocating to Owyhee County and elsewhere in Idaho. The tiny wooden wagon below sheltered Jose Erquiaga and his three loyal sheepdogs. Imagine the cultural shock experienced by young Basques who emigrated from urban areas in the old country to a sheep camp in rural Idaho. For example, when Florencio "Pancho" Aldape arrived in Boise in 1935, his employer placed him in a taxi that carried him to where his father was herding sheep. Only 14, he cried for days. When Jose Mari Artiach received his first letter at the sheep camp, he hid behind a tree and wept while reading his mother's words from Bizkaia in his homeland. (Both ISHS.)

Members of the Oinkara Basques Dancers, Inc., perform the victory dance called "Txankarrelcu" at the Basque Center in Boise in April 1964 in this photograph by Ansgar Johnson. While the Oinkara group was formally established in 1960, Basque culture and music were very much in evidence in Boise by the end of World War I. In 1917, the Basques began construction of the Church of the Good Shepherd at Fourth and Idaho Streets; it was dedicated on March 2, 1919. On May 11, the community celebration Fiesta! Music Week in the Grove Street area culminated in the final night's Promenade of Lanterns, led by the Boise Municipal Band. This procession reminded Basques of the Saint's Day parades in the old country, and in 1920 the Basques joined the Music Week festivities. The Oinkara Dancers today are world-renowned ambassadors of the Basque culture.

The 30-foot-by-6-foot mural above nearly covers a wall on a building in the Basque Block. It depicts young adults dancing, an accordionist playing, an older Basque carrying a huge granite cube on his shoulder, and, at far right, sheep leading a mule-drawn wagon. Below, the Star Hotel was a two-story Queen Anne converted to use as a rooming house from 1903 to 1975. It was a "marriage mill," where immigrant maids met many eligible Basque bachelors. The parlor had a 5¢ player piano, a handball court after 1911, and boarders shared the ground floor with the landlord's shoe shop. (Above PAP; below OBHD.)

Felipe and Juanna Arrida are pictured on their wedding day, June 12, 1915. Felipe herded sheep with his brother, Ysidro; Juanna was a house servant The men worked wherever they could, as businessmen, bartenders, in boardinghouses and pool halls, and as grocery checkers, custodians, and deliverymen. Many found employment in the company village, called Barber Town after 1906, four miles east of Boise and north of Barber Dam. In the 1920s and until the middle of the 1930s, single Basque women worked as waitresses, cooks, interpreters, and teachers. Basque wives focused on the family, cooking chorizos, eggs, kidneys, and roasts plus beans and potatoes. Basque families are closely knit and socialize among themselves. Basque women traditionally have assisted each other with everything from sewing and shopping for groceries to visiting doctors and serving as midwives.

On the left, the centerpiece of the tiny C. W. Moore Park is a replica of a large churning waterwheel; they were common along Grove Street in the 1870s. In 1891, Moore founded the Boise Artesian Hot and Cold Water Company, which heated Warm Springs Avenue mansions with natural hot water. The structure below was part of the Grove Street warehouse that dates from June 17, 1925. Today it forms part of the Basque Block, which includes a market featuring authentic Basque food, wine, and delicacies as well as a restaurant, museum, cultural center, and the 1864 Cyrus Jacobs brick residence. (Above OBHD; below PAP.)

The restaurant Leku Ona, "a fine place" in Basque, occupies a building that dates from 1905, when the *Idaho Statesman* described the Belaustegui Hotel and the Basque Boarding House built by Augustin and Petra Belaustegui as "one of the fine new buildings in Boise." Within a few years, part of the hotel became the Chico Club, a social and recreational facility for Basques and non-Basque members, including women. To join the club cost only $1, with annual dues of $1. Building owner Paxta Belaustegui and club's managers Petra and Angel Belaustegui served 35 famished guests a meal of barbequed lamb, followed by dancing. This building incorporates several Basque and community traditions, from the boardinghouse to the social club to festive entertainment that remains a hallmark of the Basque community and the Basque Block in downtown Boise. (PAP.)

Former slave Elvina "Aunt Viney" Moulton walked barefoot across the plains in 1867 until she became weary and stopped in Boise. On February 24, 1878, Elvina became the only black charter member of the Boise Presbyterian Church. She said, "Don't want to be buried from the church when I go. . . . It would be better to be buried from the undertaker's, for there might be some feeling, you know." Below, Rosalee and Warner Lewis Terrell Sr. and their children, Zenovia and Warner Jr., are pictured in Boise in 1915. The family lived on South Fourteenth Street, and Warner Jr. was a 1928 Boise High School graduate who worked as a waiter at the whites-only Arid Club. Young blacks danced at home. (Both ISHS.)

And Now We Are Visible, an original work by noted Idaho artist Marla Kriegbaum, was presented to the Idaho Black History Museum on April 24, 1998, at the office of Gov. Phillip Batt. It chronicles the black experience in Idaho from the arrival of the Lewis and Clark Expedition to Batt's sponsorship of the legislation creating the Idaho Human Rights Commission and establishing the Idaho Black History Museum. The poster also depicts blacks as miners, mountain men, loggers, builders, merchants, piece quilters, and washerwomen as well as demonstrators in front of the statehouse holding signs that read "Martin Luther King Day," "Boise NAACP 1919" and "Bill of Rights." It also illustrates the arrival of the Idaho Central Railroad branch line, a young black female scholar, and 1964 Miss Idaho USA Dorothy Johnson from Pocatello. (IBHM.)

Reverend William Riley Hardy was the first pastor of St. Paul Baptist Church

To the left, Rev. Riley Hardy was the first pastor of St. Paul's Baptist Church in 1910. By then, the pendulum of the treatment of blacks in Idaho had swung from a high in 1864, when John West, named "Dean of Colored Pioneers in Idaho," relocated from Philadelphia, to a low in 1869, when John F. Allen left Boise because he was unable to enroll his children in public schools. In 1900, there were fewer than 300 blacks in all Idaho. Below, the St. Paul's congregation began in 1909, the second black church in Idaho (the first was in Pocatello). Members were finally able to construct a building in 1921. It served the needs of the congregation for many decades until it was replaced on the site at Fourteenth and Bannock Streets and relocated to Julia Davis Park in 1998. (Above ISHS; below PAP.)

BIBLIOGRAPHY

Hart, Arthur A. *Chinatown: Boise, Idaho, 1870–1970*. Boise: Historic Idaho, Inc., 2002.

———. *Fighting Fire on the Frontier*. Boise: Boise Fire Department Association, 1976.

———. *Historic Boise: An Introduction to the Architecture of Boise, Idaho, 1864–1938*. Boise: Boise City Historic Preservation Commission, 1979.

———. *Life in Old Boise*. Boise: Taylor Publishing Company, 1989.

———. *The Boiseans: At Home*. Boise: Historic Boise, Inc., 1984.

Hartman, Hugh H. *The Founding Fathers of Boise, 1863–1875*. Boise: Idaho State Historical Society, 1989.

Johnson, Vicki S., and Patricia S. Mickelson. *Nine Walking Tours of Boise*. Boise: Boise Walking Tours, 1979.

MacGregor, Carol Lynn. *Boise, Idaho, 1882–1910: Prosperity in Isolation*. Missoula, MT: Mountain Press Publishing Company, 2006.

Oliver, Mamie O. *Idaho Ebony: The Afro-American Presence in Idaho State History*. Boise: Idaho State Historical Society, 1990.

———. *Idaho Ebony: Black Historic Idahoans*. Boise: Mamie O. Oliver, 1997.

Shallat, Todd. *Ethnic Landmarks: Ten Historic Places that Define the City of Trees*. Boise: Office of the City Historian, 2007.

Shallat, Todd, and David Kennedy, eds. *Harrison Boulevard, Preserving the Past in Boise's North End*. Boise: School of Social Sciences and Public Affairs, BSU, 1989.

Turner, Faith. *The Golden Dream. Being a Story of the Beginnings and Growth of the Public Library System in Boise, Idaho*. Boise: The Idaho Statesman, 1955.

Wells, Merle, and Arthur A. Hart. *Boise, An Illustrated History*. Sun Valley, CA: American Historical Press, 2000.

Wright, Patricia, and Lisa B. Reitzes. *Tourtellotte and Hummel of Idaho: The Standard Practice of Architecture*. Logan: Utah State University Press, 1987.

Visit us at
arcadiapublishing.com

CPSIA information can be obtained
at www.ICGtesting.com
Printed in the USA
BVHW011625221121
622226BV00005B/430

9 781531 638702